# It's a Secret for Girls!

## Password Journal Girls Edition

**Activinotes**

DAILY JOURNALS, PLANNERS, NOTEBOOKS AND OTHER BLANK BOOKS

# Password Journal

Account Name: _____

Website : _____

User I.D. : _____

Email Used : _____

Password : _____

Account Name: _____

Website : _____

User I.D. : _____

Email Used : _____

Password : _____

Account Name: _____

Website : _____

User I.D. : _____

Email Used : _____

Password : _____

*Smile*

# Notes

Password Journal

Account Name: _____

Website : _____

User I.D. : _____

Email Used : _____

Password : _____

Smile

Account Name: _____

Website : _____

User I.D. : _____

Email Used : _____

Password : _____

Account Name: _____

Website : _____

User I.D. : _____

Email Used : _____

Password : _____

# Notes

Smile

 Password Journal

Account Name: _____

Website : _____

User I.D. : _____

Email Used : _____

Password : _____

 Smile

Account Name: _____

Website : _____

User I.D. : _____

Email Used : _____

Password : _____

Account Name: _____

Website : _____

User I.D. : _____

Email Used : _____

Password : _____

# Notes

Smile

# Password Journal

Account Name: _____

Website : _____

User I.D. : _____

Email Used : _____

Password : _____

Smile

Account Name: _____

Website : _____

User I.D. : _____

Email Used : _____

Password : _____

Account Name: _____

Website : _____

User I.D. : _____

Email Used : _____

Password : _____

# Notes

# Password Journal

Account Name: _____

Website : _____

User I.D. : _____

Email Used : _____

Password : _____

Account Name: _____

Website : _____

User I.D. : _____

Email Used : _____

Password : _____

Account Name: _____

Website : _____

User I.D. : _____

Email Used : _____

Password : _____

# Notes

# Password Journal

Account Name: _____

Website : _____

User I.D. : _____

Email Used : _____

Password : _____

Account Name: _____

Website : _____

User I.D. : _____

Email Used : _____

Password : _____

Account Name: _____

Website : _____

User I.D. : _____

Email Used : _____

Password : _____

# Notes

# Password Journal

Account Name: _____

Website : _____

User I.D. : _____

Email Used : _____

Password : _____

Account Name: _____

Website : _____

User I.D. : _____

Email Used : _____

Password : _____

Account Name: _____

Website : _____

User I.D. : _____

Email Used : _____

Password : _____

# Notes

# Password Journal

Account Name: _____

Website : _____

User I.D. : _____

Email Used : _____

Password : _____

Account Name: _____

Website : _____

User I.D. : _____

Email Used : _____

Password : _____

Account Name: _____

Website : _____

User I.D. : _____

Email Used : _____

Password : _____

# Notes

# Password Journal

**Account Name:** _____

**Website :** _____

**User I.D. :** _____

**Email Used :** _____

**Password :** _____

---

**Account Name:** _____

**Website :** _____

**User I.D. :** _____

**Email Used :** _____

**Password :** _____

---

**Account Name:** _____

**Website :** _____

**User I.D. :** _____

**Email Used :** _____

**Password :** _____

Smile

# Notes

Smile

# Password Journal

Account Name: _____

Website : _____

User I.D. : _____

Email Used : _____

Password : _____

Smile

Account Name: _____

Website : _____

User I.D. : _____

Email Used : _____

Password : _____

Account Name: _____

Website : _____

User I.D. : _____

Email Used : _____

Password : _____

# Notes

Smile

# Password Journal

Account Name: _____

Website : _____

User I.D. : _____

Email Used : _____

Password : _____

Smile

Account Name: _____

Website : _____

User I.D. : _____

Email Used : _____

Password : _____

Account Name: _____

Website : _____

User I.D. : _____

Email Used : _____

Password : _____

# Notes

# Password Journal

Account Name: _____

Website : _____

User I.D. : _____

Email Used : _____

Password : _____

---

Account Name: _____

Website : _____

User I.D. : _____

Email Used : _____

Password : _____

---

Account Name: _____

Website : _____

User I.D. : _____

Email Used : _____

Password : _____

Smile

# Notes

# Password Journal

**Account Name:** _____

**Website :** _____

**User I.D. :** _____

**Email Used :** _____

**Password :** _____

Smile

**Account Name:** _____

**Website :** _____

**User I.D. :** _____

**Email Used :** _____

**Password :** _____

**Account Name:** _____

**Website :** _____

**User I.D. :** _____

**Email Used :** _____

**Password :** _____

# Notes

Smile

 Password Journal

Account Name: _____

Website : _____

User I.D. : _____

Email Used : _____

Password : _____

 Smile

Account Name: _____

Website : _____

User I.D. : _____

Email Used : _____

Password : _____

Account Name: _____

Website : _____

User I.D. : _____

Email Used : _____

Password : _____

# Notes

Smile

# Password Journal

Account Name: _____

Website : _____

User I.D. : _____

Email Used : _____

Password : _____

Smile

Account Name: _____

Website : _____

User I.D. : _____

Email Used : _____

Password : _____

Account Name: _____

Website : _____

User I.D. : _____

Email Used : _____

Password : _____

# Notes

Smile

# Password Journal

Account Name: _____

Website : _____

User I.D. : _____

Email Used : _____

Password : _____

Account Name: _____

Website : _____

User I.D. : _____

Email Used : _____

Password : _____

Account Name: _____

Website : _____

User I.D. : _____

Email Used : _____

Password : _____

# Notes

Account Name: _____

Website : _____

User I.D. : _____

Email Used : _____

Password : _____

Smile

Account Name: _____

Website : _____

User I.D. : _____

Email Used : _____

Password : _____

Account Name: _____

Website : _____

User I.D. : _____

Email Used : _____

Password : _____

# Notes

Smile

# Password  Journal

Account Name: _____

Website : _____

User I.D. : _____

Email Used : _____

Password : _____

 Smile

Account Name: _____

Website : _____

User I.D. : _____

Email Used : _____

Password : _____

Account Name: _____

Website : _____

User I.D. : _____

Email Used : _____

Password : _____

# Notes

# Password Journal

Account Name: _____

Website : _____

User I.D. : _____

Email Used : _____

Password : _____

Smile

Account Name: _____

Website : _____

User I.D. : _____

Email Used : _____

Password : _____

Account Name: _____

Website : _____

User I.D. : _____

Email Used : _____

Password : _____

# Notes

Smile

# Password Journal

Account Name: _____

Website : _____

User I.D. : _____

Email Used : _____

Password : _____

Account Name: _____

Website : _____

User I.D. : _____

Email Used : _____

Password : _____

Account Name: _____

Website : _____

User I.D. : _____

Email Used : _____

Password : _____

# Notes

# Password Journal

Account Name: _____

Website : _____

User I.D. : _____

Email Used : _____

Password : _____

---

Account Name: _____

Website : _____

User I.D. : _____

Email Used : _____

Password : _____

---

Account Name: _____

Website : _____

User I.D. : _____

Email Used : _____

Password : _____

Smile

# Notes

Smile

# Password Journal

Account Name: _____

Website : _____

User I.D. : _____

Email Used : _____

Password : _____

Account Name: _____

Website : _____

User I.D. : _____

Email Used : _____

Password : _____

Account Name: _____

Website : _____

User I.D. : _____

Email Used : _____

Password : _____

# Notes

# Password Journal

Account Name: _____

Website : _____

User I.D. : _____

Email Used : _____

Password : _____

Account Name: _____

Website : _____

User I.D. : _____

Email Used : _____

Password : _____

Account Name: _____

Website : _____

User I.D. : _____

Email Used : _____

Password : _____

Smile

# Notes

Smile

# Password Journal

Account Name: _____

Website : _____

User I.D. : _____

Email Used : _____

Password : _____

Account Name: _____

Website : _____

User I.D. : _____

Email Used : _____

Password : _____

Account Name: _____

Website : _____

User I.D. : _____

Email Used : _____

Password : _____

# Notes

# Password Journal

Account Name: _____

Website : _____

User I.D. : _____

Email Used : _____

Password : _____

Smile

Account Name: _____

Website : _____

User I.D. : _____

Email Used : _____

Password : _____

Account Name: _____

Website : _____

User I.D. : _____

Email Used : _____

Password : _____

# Notes

Smile

 Password Journal

Account Name: _____

Website : _____

User I.D. : _____

Email Used : _____

Password : _____

 Smile

Account Name: _____

Website : _____

User I.D. : _____

Email Used : _____

Password : _____

Account Name: _____

Website : _____

User I.D. : _____

Email Used : _____

Password : _____

# Notes

# Password Journal

Account Name: _____

Website : _____

User I.D. : _____

Email Used : _____

Password : _____

Account Name: _____

Website : _____

User I.D. : _____

Email Used : _____

Password : _____

Account Name: _____

Website : _____

User I.D. : _____

Email Used : _____

Password : _____

Smile

# Notes

# Password Journal

Account Name: _____

Website : _____

User I.D. : _____

Email Used : _____

Password : _____

Account Name: _____

Website : _____

User I.D. : _____

Email Used : _____

Password : _____

Account Name: _____

Website : _____

User I.D. : _____

Email Used : _____

Password : _____

# Notes

# Password Journal

**Account Name:** _____

**Website :** _____

**User I.D. :** _____

**Email Used :** _____

**Password :** _____

---

**Account Name:** _____

**Website :** _____

**User I.D. :** _____

**Email Used :** _____

**Password :** _____

---

**Account Name:** _____

**Website :** _____

**User I.D. :** _____

**Email Used :** _____

**Password :** _____

Smile

Smile

 Password Journal

Account Name: _____

Website : _____

User I.D. : _____

Email Used : _____

Password : _____

 Smile

Account Name: _____

Website : _____

User I.D. : _____

Email Used : _____

Password : _____

Account Name: _____

Website : _____

User I.D. : _____

Email Used : _____

Password : _____

# Notes

Smile

Password Journal

Account Name: _____

Website : _____

User I.D. : _____

Email Used : _____

Password : _____

 Smile

Account Name: _____

Website : _____

User I.D. : _____

Email Used : _____

Password : _____

Account Name: _____

Website : _____

User I.D. : _____

Email Used : _____

Password : _____

# Notes

Smile

# Password Journal

Account Name: _____

Website : _____

User I.D. : _____

Email Used : _____

Password : _____

Account Name: _____

Website : _____

User I.D. : _____

Email Used : _____

Password : _____

Account Name: _____

Website : _____

User I.D. : _____

Email Used : _____

Password : _____

# Notes

Smile

## Password Journal

Account Name: _____

Website : _____

User I.D. : _____

Email Used : _____

Password : _____

Smile

Account Name: _____

Website : _____

User I.D. : _____

Email Used : _____

Password : _____

Account Name: _____

Website : _____

User I.D. : _____

Email Used : _____

Password : _____

# Notes

# Password Journal

Account Name: _____

Website : _____

User I.D. : _____

Email Used : _____

Password : _____

Account Name: _____

Website : _____

User I.D. : _____

Email Used : _____

Password : _____

Account Name: _____

Website : _____

User I.D. : _____

Email Used : _____

Password : _____

# Notes

# Password Journal

Account Name: _____

Website : _____

User I.D. : _____

Email Used : _____

Password : _____

Account Name: _____

Website : _____

User I.D. : _____

Email Used : _____

Password : _____

Account Name: _____

Website : _____

User I.D. : _____

Email Used : _____

Password : _____

# Notes

# Password Journal

Account Name: _____

Website : _____

User I.D. : _____

Email Used : _____

Password : _____

Smile

Account Name: _____

Website : _____

User I.D. : _____

Email Used : _____

Password : _____

Account Name: _____

Website : _____

User I.D. : _____

Email Used : _____

Password : _____

# Notes

# Password Journal

Account Name: _____

Website : _____

User I.D. : _____

Email Used : _____

Password : _____

Smile

Account Name: _____

Website : _____

User I.D. : _____

Email Used : _____

Password : _____

Account Name: _____

Website : _____

User I.D. : _____

Email Used : _____

Password : _____

# Notes

Smile

 Password Journal

Account Name: _____

Website : _____

User I.D. : _____

Email Used : _____

Password : _____

 Smile

Account Name: _____

Website : _____

User I.D. : _____

Email Used : _____

Password : _____

Account Name: _____

Website : _____

User I.D. : _____

Email Used : _____

Password : _____

# Notes

# Password Journal

Account Name: _____

Website : _____

User I.D. : _____

Email Used : _____

Password : _____

Smile

Account Name: _____

Website : _____

User I.D. : _____

Email Used : _____

Password : _____

Account Name: _____

Website : _____

User I.D. : _____

Email Used : _____

Password : _____

# Notes

 Password Journal

Account Name: _____

Website : _____

User I.D. : _____

Email Used : _____

Password : _____

 Smile

Account Name: _____

Website : _____

User I.D. : _____

Email Used : _____

Password : _____

Account Name: _____

Website : _____

User I.D. : _____

Email Used : _____

Password : _____

# Notes

# Password Journal

Account Name: _____

Website : _____

User I.D. : _____

Email Used : _____

Password : _____

Account Name: _____

Website : _____

User I.D. : _____

Email Used : _____

Password : _____

Account Name: _____

Website : _____

User I.D. : _____

Email Used : _____

Password : _____

Smile

# Notes

Smile

**Password** **Journal**

Account Name: _____

Website : _____

User I.D. : _____

Email Used : _____

Password : _____

Smile

Account Name: _____

Website : _____

User I.D. : _____

Email Used : _____

Password : _____

Account Name: _____

Website : _____

User I.D. : _____

Email Used : _____

Password : _____

# Notes

Smile

# Password Journal

Account Name: _____

Website : _____

User I.D. : _____

Email Used : _____

Password : _____

Smile

Account Name: _____

Website : _____

User I.D. : _____

Email Used : _____

Password : _____

Account Name: _____

Website : _____

User I.D. : _____

Email Used : _____

Password : _____

# Notes

# Password Journal

Account Name: _____

Website : _____

User I.D. : _____

Email Used : _____

Password : _____

Account Name: _____

Website : _____

User I.D. : _____

Email Used : _____

Password : _____

Account Name: _____

Website : _____

User I.D. : _____

Email Used : _____

Password : _____

# Notes

# Password Journal

Account Name: _____

Website : _____

User I.D. : _____

Email Used : _____

Password : _____


Account Name: _____

Website : _____

User I.D. : _____

Email Used : _____

Password : _____


Account Name: _____

Website : _____

User I.D. : _____

Email Used : _____

Password : _____

Smile

# Notes

# Password Journal

Account Name: _____

Website : _____

User I.D. : _____

Email Used : _____

Password : _____

Smile

Account Name: _____

Website : _____

User I.D. : _____

Email Used : _____

Password : _____

Account Name: _____

Website : _____

User I.D. : _____

Email Used : _____

Password : _____

# Notes

# Password Journal

**Account Name:** _____

**Website :** _____

**User I.D. :** _____

**Email Used :** _____

**Password :** _____

*Smile*

**Account Name:** _____

**Website :** _____

**User I.D. :** _____

**Email Used :** _____

**Password :** _____

**Account Name:** _____

**Website :** _____

**User I.D. :** _____

**Email Used :** _____

**Password :** _____

# Notes

# Password Journal

**Account Name:** _____

**Website :** _____

**User I.D. :** _____

**Email Used :** _____

**Password :** _____

**Account Name:** _____

**Website :** _____

**User I.D. :** _____

**Email Used :** _____

**Password :** _____

**Account Name:** _____

**Website :** _____

**User I.D. :** _____

**Email Used :** _____

**Password :** _____

# Notes

Smile

# Password Journal

Account Name: _____

Website : _____

User I.D. : _____

Email Used : _____

Password : _____

---

Account Name: _____

Website : _____

User I.D. : _____

Email Used : _____

Password : _____

---

Account Name: _____

Website : _____

User I.D. : _____

Email Used : _____

Password : _____

Smile

# Notes

# Password Journal

Account Name: _____

Website : _____

User I.D. : _____

Email Used : _____

Password : _____

Smile

Account Name: _____

Website : _____

User I.D. : _____

Email Used : _____

Password : _____

Account Name: _____

Website : _____

User I.D. : _____

Email Used : _____

Password : _____

# Notes

# Password Journal

**Account Name:** _____

**Website :** _____

**User I.D. :** _____

**Email Used :** _____

**Password :** _____

---

**Account Name:** _____

**Website :** _____

**User I.D. :** _____

**Email Used :** _____

**Password :** _____

---

**Account Name:** _____

**Website :** _____

**User I.D. :** _____

**Email Used :** _____

**Password :** _____

Smile

# Notes

# Notes

www.ingramcontent.com/pod-product-compliance
Lightning Source LLC
Chambersburg PA
CBHW081334090426
42737CB00017B/3142